SCHIRMER'S LIBRARY
OF MUSICAL CLASSICS

Vol. 2054

FRIEDRICH SEITZ

Pupil's Concertos Nos. 1-5
COMPLETE

For Violin and Piano

Edited and fingered by Philipp Mittell

ISBN 978-0-634-09682-2

G. SCHIRMER, Inc.

DISTRIBUTED BY

7777 W. BLUEMOUND RD. P.O. BOX 13819 MILWAUKEE, WI 53213

Contents

PUPIL'S CONCERTO NO. 1

Edited and fingered by Philipp Mittell

Friedrich Seitz
Op. 7

PUPIL'S CONCERTO NO. 2

Edited and fingered by Phillip Mittell

Friedrich Seitz
Op. 13

Allegretto moderato

PUPIL'S CONCERTO NO. 3

Edited and fingered by Phillip Mittell

Friedrich Seitz
Op. 12

Violin

SCHIRMER'S LIBRARY
OF MUSICAL CLASSICS

Vol. 2054

FRIEDRICH SEITZ

Pupil's Concertos Nos. 1-5
COMPLETE

For Violin and Piano

Edited and fingered by Philipp Mittell

ISBN 978-0-634-09682-2

G. SCHIRMER, Inc.

DISTRIBUTED BY

HAL•LEONARD®
CORPORATION
7777 W. BLUEMOUND RD. P.O. BOX 13819 MILWAUKEE, WI 53213

PUPIL'S CONCERTO NO. 1

Edited and fingered
by Philipp Mittell

Violin

Friedrich Seitz

Allegro moderato

Violin

Violin

Violin

7

Violin

PUPIL'S CONCERTO NO. 2
First Position

Violin

Edited and fingered
by Philipp Mittell

Friedrich Seitz

Allegro non troppo

Violin

Violin

Violin

Violin

Violin

PUPIL'S CONCERTO NO. 3

Edited and fingered
by Philipp Mittell

Violin

Friedrich Seitz

Violin

Violin

Violin

Violin

Violin

Violin

PUPIL'S CONCERTO NO. 4

Edited and fingered
by Philipp Mittell

Friedrich Seitz

Violin

Violin

Violin

Violin

Violin

27

PUPIL'S CONCERTO NO. 5

Edited and fingered
by Philipp Mittell

Violin

Friedrich Seitz

Violin

Violin

Violin

Violin

PUPIL'S CONCERTO NO. 4

Edited and fingered by Phillip Mittell

Friedrich Seitz
Op. 15

PUPIL'S CONCERTO NO. 5

Edited and fingered by Phillip Mittell

Friedrich Seitz
Op. 22

Meno mosso